Mammals in the Wild

Chimpanzees
A 4D BOOK

by Kathryn Clay

PEBBLE
a capstone

Download the Capstone app!

- Ask an adult to download the Capstone 4D app.

- Scan the cover and stars inside the book for additional content.

When you scan a spread, you'll find fun extra stuff to go with this book! You can also find these things on the web at www.capstone4D.com using the password: chimps.00818

Pebble Books are published by Pebble
1710 Roe Crest Drive, North Mankato,
Minnesota 56003
www.mycapstone.com

Library of Congress Cataloging-in-Publication Data
Names: Clay, Kathryn, author.
Title: Chimpanzees : a 4D book / by Kathryn Clay.
Description: North Mankato, Minnesota : an imprint of
    Pebble, [2019] | Series: Little Pebble. Mammals in the
    wild Audience: Age 4–7.
Identifiers: LCCN 2018004130 (print) | LCCN 2018009136
    (ebook) | ISBN 9781977100931 (eBook PDF) | ISBN
    9781977100818 (hardcover) | ISBN
    9781977100870 (paperback)
Subjects: LCSH: Chimpanzees—Juvenile literature.
Classification: LCC QL737.P94 (ebook) | LCC QL737.P94
C55 2019 (print) | DDC 599.885—dc23
LC record available at https://lccn.loc.gov/2018004130

Editorial Credits
Karen Aleo, editor; Juliette Peters, designer;
Tracy Cummins and Heather Mauldin, media researchers;
Laura Manthe, production specialist

Photo Credits
Dreamstime: Andrey Gudkov, 19; Getty Images: DLILLC/
Corbis/VCG, 17; iStockphoto: Photokanok, 15; Newscom:
Cyril Ruoso/Minden Pictures, 13; Shutterstock: Abeselom
Zerit, 1, dmvphotos, 7, Edwin Butter, 11, Eva Lorenz, 21,
GUDKOV ANDREY, Cover, Kletr, 9, Vidoslava, Design
Element, Worakit Sirijinda, 5, Zubada, Design Element

Printed in the United States of America.
PA021

Table of Contents

Up Close

What is in the tree?

It is a chimpanzee!

Chimps are apes.

They are not monkeys.

They don't have a tail.

Chimps move.

Chimps use long arms.

They use long legs.

Mammals have hair or fur.

Chimps have hair.

Chimps are mammals.

Chimp Life

Chimps live in forests.

Some live in grasses

They sleep in trees.

Shhh.

It's time to eat.

Chimps eat insects.

They eat fruit and nuts.

Yum!

fruit

Tools help chimps eat.

They use sticks.

They use rocks.

Chimp Groups

Chimps live together.

They eat.

They play.

They rest.

A baby is born

It drinks milk.

It stays with its mother.

Glossary

ape—a large primate with no tail; gorillas, orangutans, and chimpanzees are kinds of apes

forest—a large area thickly covered with trees and plants; forests are also called woodlands

insect—a small animal with a hard outer shell, six legs, three body sections, and two antennae; most insects have wings

mammal—a warm-blooded animal that breathes air; mammals have hair or fur; female mammals feed milk to their young

monkey—a type of small animal that is related to an ape; a monkey has a long tail

tool—something used to make work easier

Read More

Kenan, Tessa. *It's a Chimpanzee!* Rain Forest Animals. Minneapolis: Lerner Publications, 2017.

Peterson, Megan Cooley. *Chimpanzees are Awesome!* Awesome African Animals. North Mankato, Minn.: Capstone Press, 2015.

Polinsky, Paige V. *Chimpanzee: Brainy Beast.* Animal Superstars. Minneapolis: Super Sandcastle, an imprint of Abdo Publishing, 2017

Internet Sites

Use FactHound to find Internet sites related to this book.

Visit www.facthound.com

Just type in 9781977100818 and go.

Check out projects, games and lots more at
www.capstonekids.com

Critical Thinking Questions

1. What are mammals?

2. What do chimps eat?

3. What tools do chimps use?

Index